EMBODIED LIGHT

Advent Reflections on the Incarnation

Melissa Tidwell

UPPER ROOM BOOKS

NASHVILLE

Cover and interior design: Nelson Kane
Cover image: Rembrandt, *The Adoration of the Shepherds*, 1646
Bridgeman Art Library International, 274 Madison Ave, Suite 1604 New
York, NY 10016. Used by permission.

LIBRARY OF CONGRESS CATALOGING-IN-PUBLICATION DATA
Tidwell, Melissa.
  Embodied light : Advent reflections on the Incarnation / by Melissa
Tidwell.
    pages cm
  ISBN 978-0-8358-1214-6 – ISBN 978-0-8358-1215-3 (mobi) –
ISBN 978-0-8358-1216-0 (epub)
  1. Advent–Meditations. 2. Incarnation–Meditations. I. Title.
  BV40.T525 2013
  242'.332--dc23

                                              2013003572

Printed in the United States of America

For my sisters

Poem

The spirit
 likes to dress up like this:
  ten fingers,
   ten toes,

shoulders, and all the rest
 at night
  in the black branches,
   in the morning

in the blue branches
 of the world.
  It could float, of course,
   but would rather

plumb rough matter.
 Airy and shapeless thing,
  it needs
   the metaphor of the body,

lime and appetite,
 the oceanic fluids;
  it needs the body's world,
   instinct

and imagination
 and the dark hug of time,
  sweetness
   and tangibility,

to be understood,
 to be more than pure light
  that burns
   where no one is—

so it enters us—
 in the morning
  shines from brute comfort
   like a stitch of lightning;

and at night
 lights up the deep and wondrous
  drownings of the body
   like a star.

MARY OLIVER

contents

introduction

D O WE REALLY HAVE TO HAVE CHRISTMAS?" I ASKED A friend this question one year when I was feeling low, not sure I had the energy for the Christmas preparations and celebrations I thought others expected of me. "Does it really matter?" My friend surprised me by responding, sharply, "Matter? Well, it's only about the thing at the very center of my being," she said. I sat up and listened. "God becoming a human being in Jesus is what my whole faith is built on. It's why I am who I am. It might matter more than Easter, really."

It took me awhile to process her answer, but it lodged in my spiritual memory bank and over the years widened and deepened into a web of interests and connections. As I read and noticed, I began to see that what my friend was talking about was the doctrine of Incarnation. It kept cropping up, the way things sometimes do when you learn about something new and suddenly see it everywhere. I stumbled across a wonderful little book called *I Believe in the Resurrection of the Body* by Brazilian theologian Rubem Alves, who says, "God's desire is revealed in our body. After all, what the doctrine of the Incarnation whispers to us is that God, eternally, wants a body like ours. Have you ever thought about this? that at Christmas what is celebrated is our body as something that God desires?"[1] Alves explores why God chose incarnation, being in flesh, as the way to reach out to creation and establish relationship, connection, a divine act of solidarity with humans and an investment in our realizing what God intends for humans to become.

Later I ran across the poem by Mary Oliver that opens this volume. The spare yet luscious lines of this poem seemed to sum up all I was thinking in a simple and powerful expression. She writes that the spirit "needs the metaphor of the body" and that the spirit longs "to be more than pure light that burns where no one is." The spirit is of a substance too marvelous for us to understand, really. We can only talk about it in metaphors, because we have no direct access to the holy itself. But if we agree to see it as light—powerful, illuminating, indestructible—then the Incarnation says that light wants to be seen.

In his film *Wings of Desire*, Wim Wenders explores another aspect of incarnation. In one of my favorite moments in this long, moody experimental German film, two angels who watch over the city of Berlin express their awed appreciation of ordinary human life—what it would mean to be embodied, to be tired at the end of a workday, to read a newspaper and have the ink rub off on one's hands.

Yet for all my appreciation of these expressions of incarnational reality, I was surprised not to find more examples of incarnation's importance expressed in writings about Christmas and Advent. And so the idea for this book began to emerge.

In the season of Advent we are asked to prepare our hearts for the coming of Christ, for this manifestation of God in human form. What Christmas proclaims to us is that God was willing to close the gap between divinity and humanity by entering into the human experience, becoming one of us, knowing hunger and thirst, friendship and betrayal, hope and loss, and the agony of death. It's a lot to take in, the implications of God incarnate. And because we can't take it in all at once, by participating in the seasons of the church year we have the opportunity to take up the idea again and again as the season rolls around to Advent. We imagine the birth of Jesus, the smells and sounds of the stable, the brightness of the star, the vulnerability of the baby, and the wonder of the shepherds. The temptation is to stop there and move on, to turn the Nativity into a sentimental tableau that has little meaning for the rest of our lives. But if we study this idea of incarnation—of Jesus being fully human and fully divine—we must consider that this event comes about because God is trying to tell us something, show us something about God's nature and about our nature, about divinity and humanity and the intersection of those two realms.

As we move through these four weeks of Advent preparations, we will consider what the Incarnation means, how it can help us know more about God and about human life. We will consider how we can experience being incarnate beings in our own spiritual practices. And we will consider the incarnate Christ and what the life of Jesus has to show us about being embodied spirits. Each day's meditation is based on a relevant scripture and includes a prayer for the day and a brief reflection question.

I pray that these meditations will move you toward considering more deeply the idea of incarnation, that of

Jesus and your own. If it leads you toward a celebration of Christmas that expresses the core of your being, I shall continue giving thanks for that conversation long ago, for my friend's keen insight, and for the love of God that shines brightly through the ages.

week one overview

IT SEEMS THAT EACH OF THE LITURGICAL SEASONS HAS its own spiritual gift, the message behind the themes we study, pray over, and assimilate. Lent places us face-to-face with sin and redemption. Pentecost blows the wind of the Holy Spirit into the early church, animating its life and giving us a time to consider our own renewal. Advent, though, has become mostly a run-up to the big celebration of Christmas, and its themes may not be at first glance as weighty as other seasons. Part of the problem is that we get a bit distracted by the idea of the baby Jesus, and babies are seldom associated with serious theological thoughts. Add to that the holly and the scent of pine, and the baking to be done and cards to write, and the distraction is almost complete. But if we persist in considering Advent apart from all the activity that accompanies it, we will see that Advent is about serious stuff, the very essence of our existence. Advent asks, "Why was Jesus born, anyway? Why were we?"

To answer that question we must look deeply into

God's divine will; God's purpose in creating the world; God's creating humans in God's own image; and God's persistent pursuit of making covenant with us, seeking to give us life and life abundant. What kind of God is this, who chose Sarah and Abraham to have a child in their aging years, who took heed of the Israelites in bondage in Egypt and brought them into freedom, who called judges and prophets to remind the people of the relationship forged in the light of that Exodus journey? And what does it mean about this God that Christ, who was present at creation, "the first born of all creation" (Col. 1:15), came to earth, fully human, fully divine?

Over the next week we will read scriptures that attest to God's activity, that suggest some potential responses to these questions. We will consider how God's desire reveals itself in Jesus of Nazareth. We use that word *desire* to imply something of God's nature: a potent force, a passionate yearning for the creation to reflect its creator, for the love and justice inherent in God's nature to be the pulse beat of the universe. And the material manifestation of that yearning is our world, with all its variety and beauty. For the sake of this world, which God loves, Jesus comes as the revealing of how human life could flower: in a life totally attuned to God's presence in the world, with no barriers of sin or alienation between Creator and created.

This week we will consider some ideas theologically, while other times we will focus more on story, poetry, and image. We will look at our own experience and that of some trusted guides. All these elements working together will, like the candles on the Advent wreath, serve to illuminate a different aspect of God's nature.

As part of the background for our work, it may be helpful as we begin this week to reflect on how you learned about God. Was it a formal process by catechism or instruction, an osmosis of ideas shared in family and church, or the result of a need to answer for yourself what this faith business was all about? What understanding of God have you assembled from these or other sources? What vocabulary seems most helpful for describing God's nature? What ideas have changed or developed as you have grown? We will touch on these questions as we progress, and they may provide interesting material for illuminating the daily reflections.

first sunday of advent

PRAY WITH YOUR BODY

CELEBRATING THE FEAST OF THE INCARNATION OUGHT to involve, at least to some degree, praying with our bodies, allowing our physical home to express its spiritual dimension. To begin, consider how you learned to pray. Many children are taught a simple prayer gesture of putting their hands together before them, palms touching. Make that gesture now, as you read. Does that posture feel more reverent? Does it carry a trace of the childlike trust in God you first knew?

Today's prayer experience will consist of an entirely wordless prayer using a series of gestures you can add to as you feel led. First, stand with your hands clasped in front of you, fingers about as high as your nose. Bow at the waist, with your hands in front of you, recognizing the presence of the Divine. Stand upright again. Slowly open your hands into a bowl shape, lowering them as you open, as if you were receiving something placed into your hands. Then pull your hands apart, stretching your arms at your sides as if preparing to receive an embrace. Raise your arms over your head, palms out, in a gesture of blessing or benediction.

Then slowly sink your hands back to your chest, bringing them back into the clasped starting position. Repeat this series of movements several times as you feel comfortable.

Now, take a few minutes to think over or write down your response to the prayer. Could you put words to each movement? How do these gestures correspond with something you know about God? What does praying with your body add to your prayer intentions?

A short video of this prayer's form, as well as other additional content is available through Upper Room Books.

Please visit the site at:

http://books.upperroom.org/book-author/melissa-tidwell/

11

to be embodied light

READ Genesis 1:1–2:1

THERE ARE SOME THINGS SO DEEP, WE CAN'T EXPRESS them in words. The flight of a hawk inspires deep silence in me, as does that moment around sunset when the light changes. There are times when a better response to an experience might involve reaching out a hand to be held by a sensitive friend or letting the tears shining in our eyes do the talking for us. Even when we do use words, the best words are not always rational, descriptive, linear sentences and paragraphs. Sometimes only poetry will do, a way of edging up on an idea, or as Emily Dickinson said, telling it slantwise. This is why the Bible starts out not with a list of rules or a history with dates and places but a liturgy, a poetic prologue.

In her poem, Mary Oliver writes about incarnation in a way that says as much to me as a stack of volumes on systematic theology. She writes first that "the spirit likes to dress up like this: ten fingers, ten toes, shoulders, and all the rest." I have read this poem out loud many times for anyone who will stand still long enough to listen, and I find I often tap my finger on my chest as I read these lines. Like this, she means, my gesture says. This body is an example of how the spirit likes to be found, out among us, not resting in some exalted temple far off in the stratosphere, guarded by six-winged seraphs—but in this humble temple, prone to head colds and hiccups, finite and temporary. Here.

Most important for the poet is that the spirit resides in temples such as this because it longs "to be more than pure light that burns where no one is." Those few words pack in a lot of meaning, an image of God that is intimate, relational, and purposeful.

What would be the purpose of God's greatness and power if they were always alone and unreachable, shrouded in mist and self-referential? God doesn't need us for completion or company, not in the way we humans need one another. But God wants us, wants connection, communion—of this I am sure. God reaches out, reaches in, shines the brilliance of holiness into our realm of the physical, and becomes embodied light, light that has form and heft, a face, a history, kinfolk and character and prayers whispered in the dark.

We see God's desire to be more than pure light in creation itself and in the history of how humans have experienced the Divine. It is an ancient story that continues right now. You can find the stories of some of our forebears in the Bible, stories of kings and prophets and farmers and mothers-in-law. In the great cloud of witnesses who have run on before us, some did great things, some were disgraceful, and many are barely remembered. You can learn a few things about what to do or not to do by reading their stories. Tragically, some people view the Bible in only one way, as a rule book or a recipe, instead of seeing it as the record of a conversation—a deep, honest, dialogue between humans and God about what it means to be alive, where God is to be found, and what makes for a life of meaning. Ultimately, I think one of the best responses to that conversation is the realization that you are its latest chapter. You are carrying on the saga, and your part in it all is to become the form of embodied light you were dreamed to become, made according to the recipe found in another immortal bit of poetry, this one by Langston Hughes:

> *Gather out of star-dust,*
> *Earth-dust,*
> *Cloud-dust,*
> *Storm-dust,*
> *And splinters of hail,*
> *One handful of dream-dust*
> *Not for sale.*[1]

~ Ask ~

What is your favorite piece of poetry? How does it convey meaning or truth in a way that other types of writing cannot?

~ Pray ~

For your creation, God of light and darkness, for hawks and sunsets and poets who give word to your mystery, we give you thanks. Give us the ability to see and respond to your movement toward deeper connection with us and through us.

cords of kindness

READ Hosea 11:1-9

THE CLASSICAL LEXICON OF WORDS ABOUT GOD, WORDS that describe what God is like, tends to be dominated by words like *omnipotent*, which means all-powerful; *immovable*, which means unchanging; and *impassible*, which means not experiencing emotions. These words convey an appropriate sense of God's glory but also can be a little alienating. They may leave us feeling that God is so big, so far away, and we are so insignificant, so tiny, that the distance between human and divine is too big to cross. And worse still, when I consider these theological words I sometimes have the guilty feeling that if a being described using these words—not experiencing emotions, not capable of change—were a person of my acquaintance, well, I wouldn't like that person very much. I would not want to spend my spare time hanging out with this person.

I think those big theological words exist to make the point that God is not a human, not like us. They remind us that God exists in categories and dimensions too big for us to grasp, so we need to stop thinking of God as someone like our grandma and more like an unmoved mover.

And yet, I find all that very hard to square up with the other thing I was taught all my life about God, that God is love. And love very much is someone like my grandma, come to think of it. In fact, I confess that sometimes in prayer when I am imagining God reaching out to me in loving forgiveness for my shortcomings, I have imagined a warmth like the warmth I experienced in my grandmother's kitchen, the peace I found in her garden, the welcome I felt as she came rushing off her porch to greet me.

My grandmother, Ruth Burns, was an anchor of stability for me. My family moved a lot during my childhood because of my father's military service, so I learned to think of home as her house, the big garden where I might get lost in the rows of corn, the stones of the sleeping porch, cool on summer nights, the sounds of my aunts and uncles singing hymns in harmony around the piano. She was always the same, always delighted to see me, always ready for a game of dominoes.

My grandmother wasn't perfect, of course. And it would be wrong to equate her with the Lord of all creation. But as a way to help my human-sized understanding begin with my own experience of love's rhythms and then from that begin to take in the love of God, I can hardly think of a better place to start.

I can imagine the voice of my grandmother when I read the words of Hosea 11. She would have felt God's anguish at the thought of giving up one of her children. She would have fought to find a way for compassion to win the day. She would have moved heaven and earth. And I think that's exactly what God did, moved heaven and earth, found a way to match ultimate justice with ultimate grace. That's why I find my new understanding of God here in Hosea 11. God, who could rightfully turn us away for our sin, refuses to do so because "I am God and no mortal" (Hos. 11:9). Divine love, which is beyond human categories, created a new avenue for the love of God to reach humanity, a new way of engrafting the whole human family into the covenant that caused God not to forsake Ephraim. It is that new way that came to us in the Incarnation, a love born in us that will lift us beyond words and into the presence of God's true essence.

~ Ask ~
When you think about God, what words or images help you connect? Which human models have been good analogies for your spiritual development? Which ones have been less helpful?

~ Pray ~
Holy One, as we seek you, help us find you, so that we can stretch mind and heart to take in the enormity of your grace and the power of your justice.

word become flesh

READ John 1:1-14

As the calendar year draws to a close, the church calendar is just beginning. The annual cycle of readings, special days, and celebrations that mark the liturgical year begins with the first Sunday in Advent. I suspect this was an intentional strategy to help believers reorient themselves in terms of time, to ask us as we worship not to be conformed to the world's time but to know, beyond our daily grind, another kind of time at work—sacred time, time that connects to our current reality but is not bound by it.

The book of John begins with this kind of reorientation. John shows us the story of Jesus in a way that connects to what has gone before but also calls for a radical shift in perspective. This begins with the book's very first words. John knows that readers of the Hebrew scriptures are familiar with the idea of the word as a means by which God expresses God's intentions. God speaks the world into creation in the beginning of Genesis, making the word *light* become actual light. And continuing through the Hebrew scriptures, when prophets are given a message, the prophet is said to receive "the word of the LORD." God's word is understood to be a series of messages in words, but also, in a deeper sense, this word is a force, a kind of deep wisdom that reveals what God intends to form and reform, establish and perfect in the created order.

In proclaiming the Word, John both connects to the Hebrew scriptures and does something profoundly new. Here, Word becomes flesh and enters into the world to transform it. John proclaims that Jesus is more than a prophet; he is an embodiment of the God who made the world and called the prophets. The message becomes the messenger.

Think about that for a moment. If we look over the course of history, we might come up with a few dozen names of individuals who so profoundly represented an ideal that they came to be the embodiment of that ideal: Abraham Lincoln, Nelson Mandela, Mother Teresa. Many of us also find it helpful to look to a hero or a kind of patron saint who embodies an ideal or teaches a way of being. We might think of Jackie Robinson, whose character was as big as his talent, or Dian Fossey, the naturalist whose deep study of gorillas helped open our eyes to environmental issues.

For Christians, Jesus is not only the symbolic life that illustrates an idea, he is the idea itself turned into a living human being. To be Christian is to take up the way of Christ, even the name of Christ, and to commit ourselves to that ongoing message. In the language of spiritual formation, we talk about having the mind of Christ, of Christ being born into our hearts. I appreciate the way Robert Mulholland puts it when he says in his book *Shaped by the Word* that each of us is a word of God spoken forth for the sake of the world.[2] God has chosen each of us to express some aspect of the divine word through our incarnation.

As Advent draws us again to consider the birth of the incarnate Word, it is a good time to think about what the living word says *to* us, spoken forth over creation, spoken forth through scripture, clothed in flesh in the person of Jesus and what it says *through* us, spoken forth in our living witness.

—⁓—

~ Ask ~

What are some of your favorite passages from the Bible? If you had to sum up their message in one sentence, what would that be? Consider writing that sentence down and carrying it with you this week as a reminder of the way the word has taken root in you.

~ Pray ~

Light of the world, who made all things, speak me afresh that I might not only hear your word and receive your essence, but also embody the word you have spoken in me.

to be more than pure light

READ Psalm 104: 1-30

WHAT IS GOD LIKE? THERE IS SOME CONSENSUS IN classical theology that we can look to three trustworthy sources. First, we can look to the Bible, recorded deeds of God's power and the unspooling of salvation history. Second, we can look to our own experience, the ways God has been present to us in the events of our lives, the events of our history and time. Finally, we can look to creation, the work of God's hands. Surely the creation reveals something of the creator, reflects the intent behind the action.

When I consider creation, the aspect that intrigues me most is the abundant diversity of life, the almost profligate variety in color, fragrance, texture, and size. There are over 400,000 different species of flowering plants. That's not counting hybrids. There are 15,000 different species of ferns alone. I could imagine 500 different types of ferns, maybe, but not 1,000—much less 15,000.[3] What sheer abundance in variety! Such richness of diversity suggests to me that the life force present in the natural order reflects the vastness of the life force in God.

When I was about ten, my family lived in the Panama Canal Zone, and I spent hours helping my mother with her small garden. She found it staggering that the hibiscus she grew there bloomed twice the size of any she had seen in the States. I expressed more interest in the wildlife, the shy howler monkeys I heard from the jungle nearby, the coatimundi and armadillos that occasionally wandered through our yard, the huge snowy egret we caught our cat in the act of trying to land as a trophy.

There I began to see the diversity of earth's landscapes and how the flora and fauna of a place reflect the uniqueness of its climate, geography, and even culture. These experiences led me to consider each aspect of nature's reality as a potential insight into the reality of God. Can we see the fingerprints of the Divine in the creative force that gave us the majesty of humpback whales and the impish delight of prairie dogs? Can we sense the spectrum of God's modes of being in the powerful leap of the leopard and the tremulous song of the plover?

Why does beauty exist? While there may be some scientific evidence of an evolutionary bias at work in plants and animals, I'm not sure that explains the gleam of the moon or the intricacy of crystals. It seems to me that nature reveals a desire for beauty, harmony, variety, and abundance. I sense the Creator's intention to express generosity, delight, passion, and joy and to give us those gifts as parts of our existence. Most of all, the beauty I see in nature suggests to me that the Creator of what we can see in the world wants to be seen, wants to be known. I think this is what Mary Oliver means when she says the spirit longs "to be more than pure light that burns where no one is."

This longing comes to us in the universe in a variety of ways, both simple and profound. It exists in the fierce insistence of the life force seen in the flower that cracks open the concrete to grow. It comes to us in this earth we know and have received to care for as responsible stewards. It comes to us, finally, in the person of Jesus, who shows what human life was created to be, how it is fulfilled, and why it matters. That is what we celebrate during Advent and what we pattern our lives around, like the slow sure progress of a sapling reaching toward the sun.

~ ASK ~

Where in the natural world do you feel closest to God? What do these places teach you about God?

~ PRAY ~

Creator God, we stand in awe of the world you have given us. Help us to see you in its glory, to know you through its goodness, and to participate in your ongoing work to make all things new.

firstborn of creation

READ Colossians 1:15-20

THE DOCTRINE OF THE INCARNATION STATES THAT Jesus was fully human and fully divine. Most of the time, I am more at ease thinking about Jesus as fully human. The Gospels give us these wonderful stories of Jesus full of the details of real human life—the meals Jesus eats with his followers, the tears he sheds over the death of a friend. These stories are immediate, concrete, real. But here in Colossians, the author of this letter makes an attempt to express something of the other side of the equation, the fully divine aspect, the identity of Christ as the second person of the Trinity, the firstborn of all creation, and the firstborn from the dead.

This passage displays theological complexity of the highest order, and probably most of us can only grope after its meaning rather than master its nuance, the way we might marvel over the discovery of the Higgs boson though the deepest details of the science are beyond us.

The Colossians text reminds me of a fascinating work of fiction, *Einstein's Dreams* by Alan Lightman, which offers imaginative depictions of the dreams of Albert Einstein. Each dream is a different world in which time operates in a manner totally unlike the way time works in our world. In one world, time runs in a circle, the same events happening over and over. In another world, time, like space, has three dimensions so every action has multiple consequences.

After reading the book, I didn't understand the theory of relativity any better in its theoretical complexity, but I did have insights into the way time acts as a force in our world, how it shapes our awareness and experiences in ways we take for granted. In that same way, once we gain an insight into incarnation, we can see it as a force in the universe, like time, that shapes our reality. It has always been there, though, like time, our understanding of it shifts as we grow in knowledge.

The author of Colossians understands Christ as the incarnating power, a cosmic first principle that holds everything together, orders the universe, and gives meaning to what results. And because this principle informed the creation of everything, it also follows that every created thing bears some imprint of the Christ in it. This is what poet Gerard Manley Hopkins meant when he wrote, "Christ plays in ten thousand places,"[4] and it may also be something physicists are discovering about the holographic nature of the universe.

But here's the thing: that Christ energy didn't just stay behind the scenes as a guiding principle or a catalyst for creation. Through the power of incarnation, the Christ energy became visible, and comes to fruition as the person Jesus of Nazareth, born as a helpless baby to a poor couple in a backwater town. This idea is so huge it is almost preposterous. If it were written as science fiction you would most likely laugh it off as too out-there to take seriously. But it's the basic idea our faith is built on, this idea of a God so intent on achieving a oneness with humanity that God enters into its history and erases the boundaries between the infinite and the limited, the thinker and the thought.

It's worth flexing our mental muscles a bit from time to time to engage the mystical language; to follow the progress of the biblical rhetoric; to try to reach its ultimate purpose, which is a reconciliation, a unity that God desires for us and thus has made possible. Even as we shake our heads at the complexity of it we can lift our hearts at its result. God is as close to us as our own breath, and Christ is the pulse beat of the eternal heart.

~ Ask ~

What does it mean to be reconciled to God? How is that like and not like being reconciled to a person from whom we have been estranged?

~ Pray ~

Holy One, even in our lack of understanding and our limited view, give us a wider imagination with which to love the world you have made, and a fuller heart through which to become agents of your reconciliation.

⌃⌃⌃⌃⌃⌃⌃
ｉ ｉ ｉ ｉ ｉ ｉ ｉ

reading the begats

READ Matthew 1:17

SOME TRADITIONS BEGIN ADVENT BY READING THE genealogy of Jesus from Matthew's Gospel, which I have heard referred to as reading the begats. This can be a trying exercise. We are tempted to skip over the tricky or obscure names. Yes, we get the point. Jesus is a descendant of David, the king. Let's move on. But we will strike gold if we persevere. The laundry list becomes liturgy, poetry even, as we move into the rhythm of the recitation, the generations from Abraham to David, from David to Joseph. We remember the stories of biblical heroes, judges and prophets, sages and sojourners. We remember that these are our ancestors too, that we are the inheritors of this tradition.

Every incarnation is story and history, a time and place, a family, a unique and unrepeatable combination of the slender threads that make us who we are. This is true of Jesus, and it is true of us. Like us, Jesus has some interesting turns in his family story. There is mention of

Tamar, who had to pose as a prostitute to trick her father-in-law into doing right by her. And if we listen carefully, we can almost hear the little cough that should accompany the honest evaluation that Solomon is David's son by—ahem—another man's wife. This is not some sanitized picture that might be presented in a public relations effort but an affirmation God's power to work through justice and inequity, success and failure, good intentions and bad.

When I was a child my family sometimes traveled to Tidwell family reunions in Alabama, where we ate amazing food and listened to amazing stories told by my grandfather. One set of stories involved some Texas kin and why they moved away. At each reunion Granddaddy asked if this was the year the Texas Tidwells would come back. I started thinking of these legendary kinfolk as one of my grandfather's tall tales, like the gold hidden in the mountain caves near his home. But years later, on a business trip in San Antonio, bored in a hotel room, I idly picked up a phone book and flipped to the page where my family name would be listed, looking for the Texas Tidwells. And to my astonishment, where I might expect in any given city to find a half dozen Tidwells listed, here there were dozens of them. Some kernels of those stories my grandfather told were probably based on real family history, maybe painful and hard but also maybe liberating and inspiring, history living in the kinfolk I never knew.

Jesus surely heard his family stories as he grew up and they no doubt influenced who he was, how he navigated his sense of time and place, his family's hopes and fears, and his own immortal destiny. Perhaps we can also learn to appreciate our own series of begats, literal and spiritual, the past that has led us here to this moment in our own history. Perhaps we are being called to break unhealthy patterns we have learned or to honor legacies of faith. Perhaps we can rectify a past injustice or start a new tradition. Whatever our particular circumstances, we can choose to make our lives a response to the gift of life we have been given, a response of gratitude and joy.

The begats remind us that God chooses to work through the stories of human beings, speaking to us in the vernacular of our day, not in spite of human nature but because of it. It is the medium God invented for the task. As we hear the names, repeated year after year, we can create a litany recognizing God's choice to work through and with our stories. It might read, "Jacob: Chosen. Tamar: Chosen. Ruth and Naomi and Boaz: Chosen." And to that list we must add our own names: Chosen.

~ Ask ~

Which of your spiritual ancestors means the most to you? If you had a chance to ask him or her a question, what would it be?

~ Pray ~

Lord, you number our days and you know our story. Give us the confidence to move forward in our lives knowing that all things—past, present and future—work for our good, through the miracles of your grace. Amen.

week two overview

THE INCARNATION IS ONE OF THE DOCTRINES OF THE church. We don't hear the word *doctrine* much these days, and it has a sort of stuffy, severe connotation, but it really only means that incarnation is a teaching of the church—one of the essential teachings that has stood the test of time.

In our first week of meditations we focused on what the doctrine of the Incarnation has to teach us about God, God's nature and will. This week our focus shifts to the other side of the equation to consider what the Incarnation of Christ teaches us about humans and human life. If Jesus is the Word made flesh, we have to ask, why flesh? Why did God choose human life as the vehicle for making a definitive statement about existence?

Human beings are, in a sense, incarnations. Not entirely, of course. Not in precisely the same way Jesus was fully human and fully divine. We are not gods. Being a human for more than a few minutes means making a mistake of some kind—forgetting to be grateful, letting our ego get in the way, being rude in traffic, having moments of greed or anger or lust. But we are spirits in the flesh, beings who must wrestle with and balance our two natures, animal and angel, human and holy. We share with Jesus in being chosen by God to bear God's likeness, image, the stamp of God's design.

Over the next week we will consider some of the implications of incarnation for human beings and how we can understand the heritage we bear in our earthly frame and in our eternal purpose. As we go through this week, it will help to ponder what messages about human nature you have received: messages about sin and brokenness, about redemption and freedom, and about the essential goodness or grossness of the human body itself. Each of these ideas plays a part in this marvelous mash-up of the human condition.

i

second sunday of advent

BODY TALK

S CRIPTURE TELLS US THAT THE BODY IS THE TEMPLE of the Holy Spirit (I Cor. 6:19). Another good translation of the word for temple in this verse is "sanctuary," which seems to suggest a place of rest, protection, safety, and care. How are things with your sanctuary? Is it well maintained and lovingly respected? Is it neglected and empty? Would a stranger passing by know there was something holy going on here, something fiercely alive?

As a prayer experience, hold a brief conversation with your body as if you were talking to the custodian of a building. Ask how it fares, what it needs, and how it contributes to the operations of the whole sanctuary. Start with your feet, since your brain usually gets top billing. Touch your feet and consider, for example: my feet are my cornerstone, the stable base from which I can engage the world. How do I care for my feet? How do I honor their role in housing my spirit? Continue up your legs, thighs, hips, belly, chest, arms, and face. Don't be too shy about this talk: your body is a divine gift, and nothing about it is shameful. Don't move too fast. Listen, and remember that you are asking God to listen in on this conversation with you.

Did you hear anything new or surprising? What came up for you as you reflected on the many connections between your physical and spiritual selves? Does this conversation suggest any action you need to take to maintain the physical side of your sanctuary? Are there any changes in attitude or awareness suggested by this conversation?

11

wonderfully made

READ Psalm 139:1-18

PSALM 139 IS A HYMN TO INCARNATION. THE PSALMIST celebrates the gift of the body, honoring it as being fearfully and wonderfully made by intricate weaving from the center of God's being. Science can describe in prose what the psalmist says in poetry. The human body is a marvel of engineering, efficiency, and design. It's incredibly strong—one cubic inch of bone can withstand a load of 19,000 pounds, yet incredibly sensitive—the nose can distinguish 50,000 different smells. It lasts for decades, shredding and rebuilding cells, while the heart beats over 2.5 billion times in an average life. And in each one of those precious days on earth our brains are directing this incredible show, with neurons that can send about 1000 impulses per second.[1]

It's amazing the things humans can do—hit a fastball, leap in a grand jeté, engineer a bridge, bake a flan. Art and science, philosophy and business, political progress and silly pictures of cats on the Internet—humans are skilled with imagination to conceive and with talents to realize our visions. To watch a great teacher at work in the classroom unlocking the structure of a new language or an actor on a stage turning herself into another human being using a few gestures and a voice is to stand in the presence of a small miracle, the combination of gift and long hard work, an apt image of the potential humans carry for what we can fashion from dreams and determination.

I recently read about a new Christmas tradition in some urban areas called "Unsilent Night" that involves a crowd in procession carrying boom boxes that play a piece of music composed for the experience. This odd celebration charms me on several levels—the quirkiness of boom boxes as a means of community celebration, the ancient ritual of procession taking place in a modern city. All of these elements, it seems to me, express a spiritual instinct, a desire of the participants to engage in community, creativity, and ritual—qualities I believe are innate yearnings placed in our souls that come as naturally to us as breathing.

Irenaeus, one of the bishops of the second-century church who helped define the outlines of Christian faith, said that the glory of God is "a human being fully alive," a phrase that inspires for me visions of an army of artists and athletes, scientists and builders, teachers and healers practicing their craft, reaching for the impossible in a quest to be their best.[2] Whether we are even aware of it, at such moments we are giving glory to God, who made us skilled and ambitious, curious and daring, persistent and adaptable. Each of these traits is a gift that reflects the majesty and tenderness of God and God's delight in what humans might become.

To be aware of the miracle that is your body inspires

gratitude and a desire to respond in some way with thanksgiving. You might respond by doing one of these great things humans are able to perform: inventing, making, and discovering. You might help another person find his or her potential by nurturing the gifts that could emerge with encouragement. The grandest use of your skill might involve being generous with your presence, using your own body as the vehicle of God's love. Go visit an older person you know is lonely, whose family might be too far away to come for Christmas. Sit with someone in the hospital. Offer a hug to someone you know who is depressed. Let your face and voice be the instruments by which the miracle of the Incarnation does its glorious work to renew the whole creation.

~ Ask ~

What aspect of being an incarnate being delights you the most? the least? As a prayer experiment, lift up the most and the least pleasant aspect of your body, and add the blessing, "Fearfully and wonderfully made."

~ Pray ~

Gracious God, giver of all good gifts, we praise you for the gift of our bodies, and for the deep and abiding knowledge you have of the whole of us, our thoughts, our needs, our innermost being. Give us the grace to know the blessings you have given us and to act in gratitude and generosity.

iii

dirt and tears

READ John 9:1-7

T HE WORD *INCARNATION* COMES FROM THE LATIN
carnis, or meat. It is an elegant way to remind us that
humans are made, basically, from meat. We're meat that thinks.
It's an outrageous idea when you see it that way, and some
believers are repulsed by the idea that Jesus was one of us in
this manner, made of meat. In fact Marcion, judged a heretic by
the early church because he would not endorse the Incarnation,
was said to have refused to accept the idea that the Lord
almighty was born into a bag stuffed with excrement.[3]

There are days when having a body seems like
Marcion's worst estimate, an unnecessarily gross burden we
must bear. To imagine that Jesus also dealt with the body's
smells and the small humiliations—that he was a baby with
a runny nose or a teenager with acne—seems bizarrely
implausible. And yet, this must be true. The doctrine of
the Incarnation demands that we affirm Jesus in the flesh,
in a body, subject to all the conditions bodies experience.

The Gospel writers have spared us most of those details, for which I thank them. But I wonder if Jesus' awareness of his incarnation is reflected in stories like the one in John 9, where he literally gets his body involved in his healing ministry, uses his own saliva to make a poultice of mud that restores sight. Jesus seems quite willing to wade into the earthy realms of spit and sweat; he doesn't shy away from the power of touch, the gift of tears, and when he is asked about the connection between sin and disease, he says quite abruptly that there is none.

Jesus' response may be related to shame, and his ability to see how shame attaches itself and burrows into the tender places of our stories and our being. Maybe he had a tender spot about his own birth story, the shame of being so poor he had to have an animal trough as his baby crib. Poor people live with a lot of shame, the constant reminders of lack and limitation and the judgment of others. And in his living closely with the poor, the sick, and the oppressed, Jesus surely saw how shame inflicted as much suffering as illness and how intertwined they could be.

At the beginning and the end of his ministry there are important stories about Jesus and water, and washing away our sins and shame. He lets John baptize him, and ever after we are baptized, cleansed. At John's telling of the Last Supper, Jesus washes the disciples' feet. In these washings, Jesus offers healing from the conditions that cause shame: sin and sickness, physical and spiritual disease, estrangement from God and from our own wholeness. Two of the churches that have significantly influenced my spiritual journey have traditions of Maundy Thursday foot-washing services. Each time I have participated in that ritual I have found it to be so moving and inspiring, but each time I have also struggled to allow myself to fully participate. There is an intimacy to displaying our poor, tired feet—the corns or calluses, or our silly baby toe—and allowing another person to show us such deep care and tenderness as he or she washes and dries our feet. Tears and hugs and deep glances of appreciation often accompany this incarnate moment of worship.

Jesus offers us redemption from shame, the chance to let his embrace of humanity wash away our deepest humiliations. Then we can embrace our life in all its messiness, even the parts our mothers taught us not to mention, and live from a sense of freedom, gratitude, and wholeness.

~ Ask ~

What memory from your past can elicit a sense of shame? Pray for God to release you from any lingering shame, and for the next few days, each time you wash your hands, repeat this paraphrase of Jesus' words from John: "That God's works might be revealed in me."

~ Pray ~

Holy One, let all who struggle with illness find strength in you, and assurance that their suffering is not a punishment but may become an avenue for grace to be made real.

family matters

READ Mark 3:20-35

B EING MISUNDERSTOOD IS A FACT OF ADULT LIFE that can wound us. The pain of it may cause us to try to warp ourselves into some inoffensive version that will make us more acceptable or marketable or easily pigeonholed into a socially understood category. We can wear ourselves out trying to meet the expectations of a boss or a parent or whoever decides what is stylish this year. But the first thing God calls us to be is ourselves, the particular blend of salt and light, history and innovation, carbon and stardust we were designed to bring forth into the world. If that leads us into places of conflict, perhaps we can receive consolation by reading this story from Mark. Jesus' family becomes concerned about him and comes to take him home. They are afraid for him. They want to protect him. But Jesus has to send them away because he is called to the path that isn't safe or predictable.

It's one of those great paradoxes of human development

that we need security and challenge, change and continuity. We need the bedrock assurance that our family is going to come looking for us if we stay gone too long; we also need the wider community of people we choose as friends and colleagues to give us alternative versions of who we are or could be.

Jesus lived with a lot of conflict. The Gospel writers frequently show him in dispute with the religious leaders of his tradition. Generations of Christian commentators have missed the point of much of that conflict and painted those leaders as the bad guys. But what I see as primary in this conflict is Jesus' sense of absolute belonging to his religious tradition. He honored it by embodying its appreciation for debate, reinterpretation, intellectual engagement, and the greater truths that could emerge from hammering out points of contention.

A friend once told me how her family lived for years with a lot of denial and secrecy about her mother's alcohol problem, using various excuses and coping strategies to cover up the bad behavior that came as a result of her mother's drinking. Shortly after my friend married, she and her new husband, Steve, went out to dinner with the family, where the predictable situation began to unfold. Except that Steve, not having long years of experience with the family system, shocked them all by refusing to play along with the usual cover-up the next day. Instead, he began a painful but much-needed conversation about the extent of the substance abuse and what kind of intervention might be needed. Some family members were initially quite angry with Steve. They thought he was the problem. Fortunately, Steve felt secure that he was part of this family and couldn't bear to see it suffering, even though the members had grown used to suffering. What eventually happened felt like a miracle to my friend when her mother agreed to enter treatment for her addiction.

Your life in God is just as securely embedded in the weave of the universe as was the life of Jesus. You belong to this family. You don't need to present some false face of piety to win God's favor or pretend to believe in some aspect of Christian doctrine that baffles you. You might even be called to push the tradition in some way, to ask if it is living up to its highest values, its deepest purpose. What delights the Creator of our varied universe is the sure unfolding of genuine faith, forged by experience and doubt, blunder and triumph, time and eternity. Expressing your incarnation, your gift, your voice, is a way to give thanks for the particularity of your existence, the singular quality of your being.

~ Ask ~

In what part of my life—family, work, church, community—do I feel the most understood and accepted? Where does the most conflict lie? What would it mean if I could understand the conflict as a gift?

~ Pray ~

God of deepest knowing, thank you for understanding us and loving us for all our complexity. Help us grow into our awareness of our place in your world and take up our call with confidence and charity. Amen

heirs and joint heirs

READ Romans 8:14-27

IN THE TIME OF JESUS, PEOPLE LIVED IN TIGHTLY connected webs of family kinship. Sons inherited wealth in birth order according to a complicated but ironclad set of rules. A number of biblical stories hinge on questions of patrimony and inheritance, the rights of children to receive their legacy and the consequences if the order is not maintained. Think of Jacob, tricking Esau out of his birthright. Think of the prodigal son, asking for his share of the estate before his father's death.

Today's passage from Romans uses the language of law and inheritance to make a startling and original claim: Those who follow Jesus are now the joint heirs of the kingdom that Jesus stands to inherit from his heavenly parent. It means we are family, connected, and as such we have certain rights and responsibilities. We share a certain spiritual DNA with Jesus. Like him, we have a share in the divine nature. We are made in the image of God, and nothing can deprive us of this inheritance of eternal value.

If you reflect for a moment, you can probably make a short list of the things you inherited from your family, not so much the material ones but the talents, interests, traits, tendencies. As we take stock, we might lament over some of these things. Like my father, I am prone to certain kinds of grandiose daydreaming and procrastination—while others are the happy gifts, like having a green thumb or a nice singing voice. Each of us is a cauldron of these inheritances, for better or worse.

Certain strains of our faith seem to harp overmuch on the concept of original sin and the low estate of our mortal nature. Tons of gloomy hymns describe humans as worms, as cursed, as wretched failures bound for damnation. And they are not totally wrong about our propensity for sin or our weakness. We need to be reminded regularly that we are not God, that we don't get to control the universe. But when overemphasized, that kind of thinking can lead us into an error on the other end of the scale. We can begin thinking that human life doesn't matter at all, that it is disposable, meaningless, even contemptible. We warp Christian theology when we fall into the trap of attempting to glorify God by denouncing humanity. The Incarnation provides a corrective, a doctrine that declares we are worth more than contempt. It says we have a share in the kingdom.

We may find this hard to believe on days when we are painfully aware that we do not feel like or act like a perfect image of godliness—those days in the pre-Christmas bustle when we are anxious and annoyed and wish the whole thing would just pass on by without our having to be involved. Or those days when we know our decorations won't look as good as the neighbors or our gifts won't be as nicely wrapped as our sister's or our turkey won't be as moist as the television chef promised. But despite the many ways we feel we don't belong, measure up, deserve, or fit in, Jesus says we have a share of the kingdom. And this share was given to us not because of anything we might do or earn or buy but because of our very nature, our kinship. We share family connection with Jesus through incarnation, and we wear it in our bodies every day, a sign and symbol of our belovedness.

~ Ask ~

What does kinship in your family mean? The inheritance of a history, a set of stories, certain physical traits? What would you like to pass on as your legacy?

~ Pray ~

Jesus, dear brother, thank you for bringing us into your family and sharing your inheritance with us. When we feel worthless, remind us that we matter to you.

the work of your hands

READ Psalm 8

THE INCARNATION MEANS THAT GOD CHOSE TO ENTER human life as an ordinary human being in Jesus of Nazareth. It means that God goes to great lengths to be close to us, which discloses God's loving nature that is always reaching out, always drawing us close.

Incarnation also says something about human life. To believe that God chose to come as one of us challenges some of the more severe viewpoints of humanity's worth. Rather than seeing human life as eternally cursed by virtue of original sin, perhaps incarnation means we are perpetually blessed, given a special relationship with God and related by birth to Jesus, who shared in our human nature and elevated its history.

Some people feel okay about that idea in the abstract; it applies to the idea of human life in general or for other people who deserve it. But to proclaim our own body as precious or valuable—many of us find this hard to do. We judge ourselves against impossible standards of beauty. We see our imperfections more clearly than our radiance. When we consider our own body, we focus on the flaws, the ways in which we do not measure up. Maybe we see a nose that's too big or legs that are too skinny. We see the hair we inherited from the wrong side of the family, and we wonder why we couldn't have looked more like our mother, why our sisters got the beauty genes. We see the signs of aging, gray hair, wrinkles, and long for the vigorous days of youth. We refuse to believe that our body could be something God chose, celebrates, loves. We have scars, infirmities, chipped teeth, weak lungs. We face our bodies with shame and regret and fail to see the spiritual in the physical.

It seems remarkable, inconceivable that God chose flesh as the avenue for expressing divinity. Why flesh? Flesh is not easy. Flesh hurts. Flesh struggles against flesh even to be born. Flesh spends years throwing up and falling down. Flesh spikes temperatures and catches chicken pox. Flesh erupts in acne and is invaded by flesh-eating bacteria. Flesh bleeds and burns. Flesh fails. Flesh forgets. Flesh falls prey to cancer and dementia, to brain tumors and heart attacks. Flesh wears out eventually. Then flesh disintegrates and after a while is gone forever from the face of the earth. Flesh is feeble and finite and forgotten.

And yet God, who could have anything God wanted, chose flesh.

The Incarnation insists that we cannot totally separate the spiritual and the physical. We are made in God's image, bearing God's likeness. The psalmist asks in wonder how humans are even worthy of God's attention and yet goes on to proclaim that the human being was given a crowning glory, a special place in the created order just a little lower than the angels. It is exactly this paradox that makes human life so confounding and intriguing. Perhaps the limitations of our flesh inspire us to strive; the awareness of our finitude makes us embrace life's sweetness.

When we look in the mirror, what looks back at us is the way God chose to enter history. The way God chose to be known, to reach out to us across the divide. Can that thought make you more tender toward the face you see reflected there? Perhaps Advent is a time to celebrate incarnation by practicing forgiveness of your own physical flaws and honoring what you have in common with Jesus. Compose a prayer today of thanksgiving for your body, for the features you like and the ones you don't, for the miraculous machinery that makes up part of who you are and through which God chooses to bless humanity.

~ Ask ~

What is your best, most beautiful feature? Your least? How can you regard all your physical life as a gift?

~ Pray ~

Loving God, we praise you for incarnating your spirit in our body. Help us to feel the love that made us and to let that love be reflected in the face we present to the world. Amen.

ʌ ʌ ʌ ʌ ʌ ʌ ʌ
i i i i i i i

annunciation

READ Luke 1:26-37, 46-56

THE STORY OF THE INCARNATION BEGINS WITH pregnancy as Mary becomes a vessel for the Holy Spirit, a partner in the creation of new life.

Pregnancy creates a whole series of physical and emotional changes in a mother-to-be. Some women thrive, while others suffer all kinds of complications. It's a universal condition with permutations that make each experience unique. And though it is one of the most personal human experiences, it is not a private one. Pregnant women are a visible sign of new life. People respond to pregnancy. They offer home remedies for morning sickness, share their labor stories. They speculate about the gender of the coming child. They even sometimes ask to touch the belly of the pregnant woman, hoping to feel a kick from the developing child. This is probably not fun all the time. Doubtless, pregnant women sometimes feel their partnership in new life is a vastly unequal one, and they wish they could get a day off.

Living a life of faith is, in a sense, being pregnant, agreeing to be a vessel for the Spirit, a partner in the creation of new life. Our spiritual pregnancy might cause us to glow with well-being, but it will also cause us to suffer as we come to grips with the things our faith asks of us that are hard, messy, and even risky. And it can be uncomfortably public. It will not be fun all the time. And at times we will feel that we are doing all the heavy lifting and wish we could just take a day off.

Over time our partnership in faith will start to bear fruit. Something will be born from our pregnant faith, and it will grow in ways we could never have imagined. Just like a baby, it may not emerge looking all that beautiful, but it is precious in the eyes of its Creator. And as it grows, certain features will emerge; certain traits that may surprise us, delight us, confound us, as we try to understand what we have created, nurtured, discovered. We will feel new parts of our faith emerge, learn that we are capable of forgiveness and trust in ways we didn't dream were possible. We will see the world differently considering the love we have experienced. And we will want to offer tangible expressions of that love.

It's not clear to me how much choice Mary had in her role as the mother of Jesus, but the Magnificat suggests that once she understood some of what it meant, she assented with her whole heart to God's audacious plan. It's not always clear to me how free will works and what it means to be called by God before our conscious awareness. The prophets suffered under the burden of election to their task. Jeremiah, in one terrible moment of doubt, likens it to an assault. And yet seeing what redemption might arise from the work he is called to do, Jeremiah assents to God's relentless call (Jer. 20).

Our work of partnership with God may never bring about words as divine as the Magnificat or as prodigious as Jeremiah's. We may not even know in our lifetime what our greatest work was, how far its reverberations were felt. As we are stretched and filled and emptied by the power of the Spirit, our call is to be faithful to the particular arc manifest in the pregnancy of our belief, to hope and pray that we have the courage to face its demands and a heart strong enough to bear the love we carry.

~ Ask ~

Is there a favorite song or hymn that you would sing to God as an assent to the task God has chosen you for? Find a time today to sing it, either silently or aloud.

~ Pray ~

Let my soul magnify you, Lord, and rejoice in you. Bring about in me the promise of new life.

week three overview

IN THE PREVIOUS WEEKS' READINGS, WE HAVE LOOKED at the Incarnation from two different angles, examining what it reveals about God and God's divine purposes as well as what it reveals about human life. In this section, our meditations will consider the implications of the Incarnation for daily living. What are we called to do and become if we wish to honor the Incarnation, to embrace its theological implications?

We are guided in this question by what Jesus did and said, how he led the disciples and carried out his earthly ministry, and how his early followers reflected in the Gospels and Epistles on what it is to continue living the Jesus way.

This way seems to be summed up in Jesus' answer to a question about what we must do to inherit eternal life (Luke 10:25-37). Jesus describes the call of God as a two-fold path: to love God with all our heart, mind, spirit, and strength and to love our neighbor as our self. Learning to love God is not simple; it is not an emotional conversion that happens once and never recedes. Rather, learning to love God is a lifelong process, a pattern of seeking, finding, and attending to mystery. Learning to love our neighbor is also a process, and it seems to begin with the question Jesus is asked next—who is my neighbor? This question is more complex than it might seem, and Jesus does not answer the question simply. Instead, he tells a story that challenges us to begin seeing God in the stranger, making peace, giving freely. Such acts lead us into wider and wider patterns of God's radical inclusivity, drawing all people toward God's deepest purpose.

We can see much of Jesus' ministry—and the ministries of those who want to follow him—as related to incarnation: a cluster of activities that honor the body by feeding the hungry, healing the sick, siding with the vulnerable, and seeing God in the face of the ones Jesus called "the least of these" (Matt. 25:40).

Readers will note that the title headings on each of the daily meditations in this week are short imperative sentences. They are meant to echo Jesus when, at the end of this discourse, he told his listeners, "Go and do likewise" (Luke 10:37).

third sunday of advent

WALKING PRAYERS

P RAYER IS NOT ONLY AN INDIVIDUAL ACT; IT IS ALSO communal. We pray for and with others and so are united in the body of Christ into a mystical communion that stretches the boundaries of space and time. Today our body prayer involves praying for our neighbors—not only in the general sense but in the most practical and specific sense.

If at all possible, take a walk around your neighborhood today. As you walk by each dwelling, say a prayer for the neighbors there. Pray for their protection and safety, their peace and health, their family life and relationships. Pray that they experience a joyous Christmas and blessings for the coming year. Bless their pets or their gardens, their vocations and their hobbies. If you know them, use their names and bring their faces to mind as you pray. Pray for the neighborhood as a whole, for peace between neighbors, for the flourishing of a healthy sense of community. Pray for the earth itself, for the trees and the birds and the many varied forms of life represented in the surrounding ecosystem.

When you finish your walk, take a few moments to

consider the process. Were you able to experience it as a form of prayer? What other forms of communal prayer have you experienced? How was this the same? Different? What did the walking and being physically present add to your experience? Did it detract anything? How would you respond if you knew someone was praying this way for you?

11

go deep

READ Luke 5:1-9

THE ROMAN PLAYWRIGHT TERENCE, WHO LIVED AROUND two hundred years before Christ, wrote a play about fathers and sons seeking to understand one another. When Chremes asks Menedemus how things are going, at first Menedemus tries to brush the question off, saying it isn't really his concern. But Chremes isn't deterred so easily. "I am a man," he replies, and therefore, "nothing that is human is foreign to my interests."[1]

This remarkable statement of solidarity with all human experience is what Jesus achieved when he crossed the boundaries of his clan to heal the child of the Syrophoenician woman or when he asked for water from the Samaritan woman. Even though multiple boundaries separated him from these women, boundaries of race and tradition, boundaries of how men and women in his day were expected to interact, Jesus did not avoid the conflict but resolutely embraced all those who suffer.

Jesus cast out demons from the Gerasene demoniac, a man whose suffering was so grotesque the townspeople had to exile him to a cemetery, where they chained him up so he would not wreak havoc in the village. No one is too disgraceful for Jesus, too ugly or hateful or too far gone. He ate with prostitutes and tax collectors; he told approving stories about a scheming accountant and the unfair wages paid by a crazy liberal farmer. He caused a lot of people to be terribly upset with him, so much so that he felt compelled to add at the end of one of his sermons, "And blessed is anyone who takes no offense at me" (Luke 7:23).

The early church had trouble sorting out the practical implications of this wideness and inclusivity. At times it threatened to split them apart, but time and again the Spirit somehow led them to find accommodation, to offer wise ways to be true to our tradition and to welcome those with other traditions, to not fear diversity of practice, to not fear at all. The current church still has trouble understanding Jesus' radical ideas and who we should understand our neighbor to be.

Perhaps it was possible for Jesus to love the people he encountered, however unlovable they might seem to us, because he, like Terence's character Chremes, was able to see some deeper humanity present even in the most wounded and scarred. Perhaps his vast spiritual powers included the grace of seeing in those around him not the disfigurement their sin or sickness had wrought but the mark of God's design still faintly visible, the traces of their incarnation.

In *The Last Battle*, the final installment of C.S. Lewis's Narnia Chronicles, the young followers of Aslan race deeper and deeper into the Narnian landscape, urged on by the cry, "Further up and further in."[2] After the final defeat of evil forces, they discover that Narnia is bigger, more expansive than ever. They keep expecting to come to the end of the territory, the limits of Narnian land. But this Narnia doesn't work like other places. It has no limits. The deeper they are willing to explore in the new dynamics of this place, the more there is for them to discover. The further into the kingdom they go, the more of it there is.

What would it mean for you spiritually to cast off every limitation you have known, to respond to the wild and unpredictable summons of the Spirit that calls you to go further up and further in?

Cast your nets deeper, Jesus urged Peter after that long-ago night of fishing on the lake (Luke 5:1-5), and he urges us now to go deeper, to search wider, to open our arms without fear to embrace the world God made for us and the humanity Jesus was born to redeem.

~ Ask ~

Which of the parables of Jesus do you like the most? Which do you like the least? What point does the parable make that leads you to wish Jesus had left this part out? What would you have to do to embrace that message?

~ Pray ~

Jesus, we love you. We aren't so sure about some of your friends. Help us to see the world through your eyes and to love it through the grace you give.

iii

face temptation

READ Matthew 4:1-11

I T'S TRADITIONAL TO READ THE STORY OF JESUS IN THE wilderness at the beginning of Lent, but considering the meaning of temptation is also instructive in Advent.

Jesus faces a series of temptations in the wilderness that presented questions for him about how he will use his power. To fill his own needs? To be rich and famous? Will his human need for food outweigh his spiritual need to be in prayer? Will his divinity be so overwhelming that he stops living by the physical laws of human boundaries? Does he even need God anymore?

When we live the incarnate life, we face questions about how we will use our power—the power of our physical selves, perhaps known in our sexuality; the power of our spiritual selves, known in the temptation to be self-righteous; the power of our social selves, found in our wealth or intellect or creativity. Do we really need God? Does God need us?

Jesus faces down the temptations by staying in alignment with who he is and what he has been sent to do. He can then move out of the wilderness and toward the work for which he was born. But I don't think Jesus faced these temptations one time and then was done with all that. The Gospels often picture Jesus going off alone to pray and meditate, to realign himself with his purpose. Jesus drew strength from his inner life to face his outer life.

We know all too well stories of those who lost a battle with temptation. We can think of political figures or movie stars or athletes we have admired who fell from grace, gave in to corruption or addiction or greed. We might find it harder to think of examples of those who withstand temptation, who struggle and triumph. Such struggle goes unheralded: it isn't news when a person votes his or her conscience, stays out of trouble, makes good decisions. It doesn't seem heroic, but it is. Reflect, for example, on the epic journey Frodo and Sam take to destroy the ring in *The Lord of the Rings*. It involves a series of tests and battles, hardships and awakenings, but their goal differs from many heroes' journeys—it is a journey not to get power but to give it up. Throughout their trek, Sam and Frodo must resist the temptation to give in to evil and appropriate the power of the ring for their own designs.

Sometimes the Advent path can be cluttered with too much holly and red bows and too many parties and errands and blaring music. We can be pulled and distracted by our busyness and others' needs. And if we are really honest, we admit that temptation can lurk there: to make the season a misuse of our resources; to paper over a dried-up relationship with an extravagant gift; to force the kids into stiff clothes so we will look good arranged in the pew; to go through the motions rather than engage our heart.

Resisting such temptations hardly seems like part of the epic struggle of good and evil. But each little struggle with the temptation to deny our spiritual path forms part of that big story of how grace faces down the power of death.

The good news is that a place of quiet and emptiness exists, and that even a few minutes there can clear our head and remind us of who we are and what we are called to do. The Spirit will lead us out to the desert, where we can face down our fears and realign ourselves with our real purpose. Then the angels come and guide us to the place where we are needed to make the kingdom come.

~ ASK ~

What is the greatest temptation you have faced? How does it relate to some aspect of your personal power? How does the temptation represent a distortion of your spiritual gifts?

~ PRAY ~

Give us places of silence and emptiness in which to face our temptations. Let us not fear them, but boldly claim our spiritual resources to see through them and the hollow falsehoods on which they are built.

𝚤 𝚤 𝚤 𝚤

practice hospitality

READ Hebrews 13:1-6

YEARS AGO I STUMBLED INTO A LITTLE CHURCH IN Atlanta called Clifton Presbyterian, which had undertaken a remarkable ministry by opening the doors of the church and inviting homeless men to come inside. When I first visited there, I saw that there were no pews in the sanctuary, just a circle of folding chairs. The church had removed the pews to make room for the homeless guests. Seeing this made the word *sanctuary* mean something real to me.

When I worshiped in that space, the stack of foam rubber mattresses piled up in the corner and the smell of lunch cooking in the kitchen made me feel close to God like no other place did. It was sometimes noisy and chaotic, and the roof leaked. The congregation was very small, and resources were strained. But it was a school for holiness to me.

Clifton's guiding principle in ministry was hospitality, the idea that when we feed a hungry person we are extending a spiritual value, welcoming the stranger, who just might turn out to be an angel in disguise. Clifton's founders learned that homelessness is a social problem related to complex issues: addiction, mental illness, housing, employment, gaps in the social safety net. Our church couldn't fix those problems, but we did not despair in making the attempt to love the people who found their way to us and to show them God's hospitality.

Hospitality comes from the Greek word *philos*, an expression of fraternal love, and *xenos*, which can mean both guest or friend and also stranger or alien. (This is where we get the word *xenophobic*.) When we show hospitality, we are making a friend out of one who might be a stranger. Some of the homeless guests we met at Clifton were a little scary and alien at first. But as we practiced hospitality, they became friends, even family.

The spiritual practice of hospitality is direct, immediate, hands on. You can't outsource it. It's about presence, looking another human being in the eye and showing that you care, that you understand how we are all related and interdependent. We can't pay back the love we have been given much of the time, so we pay it forward, pass it on, trusting God to work out the details if we show up with hot coffee and a warm heart.

Jesus spent a lot of time going from place to place, and he was fed and sheltered in a web of hospitality that perhaps seeped into his preaching and teaching. He told many stories about banquets and weddings and out-of-town guests, and if you read his stories with his travel experiences in mind, hospitality seems to be a key to unlock a vision of God: Generous bosses who pay more than a fair day's wage; generous Samaritans who care for their mortal enemies; generous fathers who don't disinherit the sons who kind of deserve it.

In the post-Resurrection story about Jesus meeting the disciples on the road to Emmaus, they fail to recognize him until they eat together. In the breaking of the bread their eyes were opened. As we eat and drink with family and friends over the next few weeks, let us pray that our eyes will be opened to the presence of Christ among us in the faces of our family and friends and coworkers and neighbors. It may be that the Christ will come to us once again in a form we don't expect—not as the one who makes us feel the best but as the one we didn't see or hear until the blessing of Christ transformed our vision.

~ Ask ~

When have you experienced hospitality? When have you been able to extend it? Why did it matter to Jesus? Why does it matter to you?

~ Pray ~

Christ, our host, our guest, help us as we seek to live with the generosity and hospitality you taught us, and to welcome you in the strangers you send us.

befriend god

READ John 15:12-17

WHEN SOMEONE ASKS JESUS WHAT THE GREAT commandment is, he offers this summary: we are to love God with all our being, all our heart, mind, soul, and strength, and to love our neighbors as ourselves (Mark 12:28-33). This Great Commandment sets forth an amazing statement of what embodied faith is to be and do. We can look to it again and again and still learn more. It seems the simplest and yet it is the hardest, mostly because it is not about doing certain things, following certain rules, minding prohibitions but about the condition of the heart, about love. It's hard to will your way into love, to make love into a daily routine like an exercise regimen or a new diet. We experience love in relationship, not abstraction. And yet for many of us, God is an abstraction at best and at worst a feared tyrant who constantly threatens punishment and eternal torment for those who don't get it right. If you weren't raised with such an idea of God you are incredibly lucky.

For those of us who were raised with such an idea, loving God—which begins with trusting God—can be a tough task.

But even if you don't face the difficulty of fearing God, there can also be the difficulty of God's remote nature. No one has seen God or has the sound of God's voice in her or his memory bank to draw on. The incarnation of Christ offers us a human life to give shape to God's nature and illustrates in vivid pictures what we seek to know about God. Jesus performed miracles, and we can study them. Jesus told stories, and we can repeat them. Jesus had relationships, and we can emulate them for our lessons in love.

You can see Jesus' love in his patient dealings with his disciples. I have sometimes wondered about Jesus' choice of the disciples, who at times in the Gospels seem so obtuse, so clueless, that it is hard to see why he kept them around. The disciples had seen Jesus work miracles. Maybe at first they hoped he would work a miracle for them. Perhaps they thought that by association, he would make them wealthy or important. But as the days and months went by, what developed between the disciples and Jesus was something else, something close enough that Jesus tells them in their last meal together that he no longer sees them as his servants but as his friends.

We too might first approach our friendships from the desire to get something for ourselves that we need. Our friends balance us and mirror us; they help us try out ideas, imagine new hairstyles and professions, and shape the contours of our identity.

When we base our relationships on trust and not fear, when we give of ourselves without calculating what we will get in return, we are obeying Jesus' commandment to love one another. And we go one step more: we are becoming friends of God.

Being a friend of God doesn't mean we are now so chummy with the Lord that we can forget about awe and reverence or give up prayer and spiritual disciplines in favor of the occasional text message. It means that our obedience to the Great Commandment is now based on a new level of trust, intimacy, and maturity. It means that those things we once understood as rules or commandments are now part of our deepest will and our deepest joy.

~ Ask ~

How has friendship contributed to your development as a person? as a follower of Christ? What distance do you need to close before you can know God as a friend?

~ Pray ~

Loving God, thank you for the friendships that sustain us. Give us the strength to be perceptive and faithful, honest and kind, and to love others as you have loved us.

ʌ ʌ ʌ ʌ ʌ ʌ
i i i i i i

be poor

READ Luke 12:22-31

IN THE FIRST WORDS OF JESUS' SERMON ON THE MOUNT, he says, "Blessed are the poor," and from that day to this people have scarcely stopped trying to decode or recode his message. It isn't easy because Jesus spoke in terms that were both practical and metaphorical, aimed at certain individuals and aimed at all who would believe. It takes study and faith to find the balance of his message, a willingness to weigh and compare and discern the context of Jesus' ministry and the context in which we live.

It seems that Jesus is speaking on at least two levels. He first warns about the dangers of wealth, the way possessions can become the master instead of the servant and the vigilance needed to avoid idolatry. You can't serve God and wealth, Jesus says. A hard saying. Note that each time Jesus delivers a hard message about money, he does so with compassion, reassuring us that God knows we have needs for food and clothing. Don't be anxious, he tells us, realizing that worrying about money surely creates anxiety.

The other level on which Jesus refers to wealth is the spiritual level, with poverty as a metaphor for emptying the self before God. When Jesus says the poor are blessed, what does he mean? I believe Jesus is saying that poor people have fewer illusions and self-deceptions about the state of their existence. If you are poor, you know it. You know you need help. And it's at that moment, when we admit the poverty of our spirit, when we know we need help, that God can overcome our pride and our shame and lift us out of our suffering.

These two levels of understanding are interdependent. We can't find true poverty of spirit if we are wallowing in gaudy luxury. Luxury has a way of taking over, distracting us from everything except its own glittering image. And it's pretty tough to serve God rather than wealth unless you have done the spiritual work that supports a change in lifestyle. Otherwise it becomes an empty act of economic management.

A friend told me recently about the hilarious experience of watching her two dogs tussle over some toys. They seemed to want to play with their toys and simultaneously guard them against the other dog. If one dog approached, the two might play together for a moment. Then, apparently realizing that they were leaving their pile of toys unguarded, they would race back to defend the loot. Neither dog could grasp that as long as they were playing with their rival, she could not possibly be making off with the toys, or, for that matter, that the toys weren't really their private property to begin with. This sums up the situation we humans deal with every day regarding our possessions, our money, our status, our credit ratings, our salaries, and our parking spots. We can never simultaneously defend and enjoy our stuff. It's much more fun to share. And none of it truly belongs to us in the first place.

We live the Christian life, the life of incarnation, in a holy balance, a fleshing out in our experience of the spiritual and the material—not in some constant warring struggle but in a union, a completion, a prayerful integration. We don't know its true achievement in a day or a season but rather in the slow and honest process of bringing our priorities in line with our values, with what we are called to become and give to the world. When we align with God's economy, we are promised a lack of anxiety, a knowing, and a sense of blessedness. This is what it means to inherit the kingdom.

~ Ask ~

What experiences have most shaped your views about how much material wealth you need? What experiences have shaped your spiritual view of money? Are these ever in conflict? If so, how do you resolve that conflict?

~ Pray ~

Praise God from whom all blessings flow. Give us the wisdom to see all we have as a gift from you and the generous spirit to share with those who need our help.

forgive and be forgiven

READ Matthew 6:9-15

THE LORD'S PRAYER SETS THE PATTERN FOR THE Christian life. It is remarkably simple and remarkably deep. It reminds us what it means to be in right relationship with God, to seek God's will. It also reminds us what it means to be in right relation with others—to ask for only what we need, not more, and to link our sense of forgiveness with our need to forgive others. Whether you say *debts* or *trespasses*, the point is the same. Forgive us as we forgive.

Forgiving borrows the vocabulary of commerce, of banking and bookkeeping. If people have wronged you, they owe you a debt. They owe you some act of restoration to put things right. At the very least they owe you an explanation and apology. Until that happens, you hold the debt and mark it in your account ledger as unpaid. In accounting terms, a debt someone owes you is called a receivable, something you have the right to receive. And receivables are assets to the person who holds them; the more people owe you, the better off you are. Holding a lot of debts increases your wealth. But in God's economy, an unforgiven debt becomes a *toxic* asset. Holding on to it is not an asset, it's a liability. It will pour poison into your heart and eat away at your core like acid. Getting rid of the debt is the only way you can keep the corrosive effect of resentment and hostility from doing its worst.

At its root, refusing to forgive is a form of idolatry. We claim that our sense of having been wronged counts more than God's, that we are somehow a better judge of character than God is. By forgiving the people who have wronged us we hand them and their intentions, actions, and results over to God. We may find this hard to do if we suspect that God is not going to be nearly as tough on our debtors as we would be. Grace may seem soft and forgiveness naïve, while we remain righteous. It can be difficult to let go of this role of righteous avenger. It feels strong and in control. The problem is that it is based on a lie. We're not more righteous than God. We don't know the interior of others' hearts. We don't have a monopoly on the truth.

True forgiveness doesn't simply relinquish the past, it invests in a different future. At the heart of Victor Hugo's *Les Miserables* lies the story of the thief Jean Valjean who is taken in by a bishop. When Valjean is caught trying to steal the bishop's silver, the bishop takes a remarkable stance: he insists that the taking of the silver was not a theft but a gift, and he urges Valjean to use this forgiveness to improve his life. That act of forgiveness and trust has a ripple effect through the rest of Valjean's life. It causes him to become a person who sacrifices himself of behalf of others.

We can let go of our role as the self-appointed judge by remembering honestly what it feels like to be a debtor, to owe a debt we can't repay. Only because God will forgive us can we bear our own burden of debts. Once we know how much we owe, we can start to release some of what we are owed. And once we can forgive, we can actually feel our own forgiveness take root and bear the fruit of freedom. It's a gift you give yourself by giving to someone else. It costs nothing but is worth everything.

~ Ask ~

What feels harder—forgiving others or forgiving yourself? What do you need to release in order to let forgiveness become a reality?

~ Pray ~

Teach us to forgive as you forgive, gracious God. Teach us to love as you love. Let us see in ourselves and in others the traces of your presence.

week four overview

I N THE FINAL WEEK OF ADVENT, OUR ATTENTION TURNS to the grand feast day that has been approaching. Considering the insights that have accumulated over the past three weeks, how might we let our awareness of the Incarnation inform our celebration of Christmas?

Many Christians feel highly conflicted about Christmas. It is a big, joyous, wonderful day. Yet it has gotten muddled for some of us by materialism and secular hoopla. We may find it difficult to sort out which parts of the traditions we follow truly promote our spiritual values and which ones subtly undermine them; which elements help us celebrate the Incarnation and which elements get in the way.

Take Christmas trees, for example. It is probably true that the origin of this tradition comes from some long-ago pagan observance that the early church borrowed to make Christmas more comprehensible to the groups it sought to evangelize. But the tradition as we have received it is deeply symbolic of the Christ story. We use an evergreen to symbolize the eternal, always growing, ever new nature of our eternal life. We decorate the evergreen with lights to echo the Gospel declaration that "The light shines in the darkness, and the darkness did not overcome it" (John 1:5). We add to the tree other symbols of the things we find beautiful: stars and angels, snowflakes and animals. Yes, it's a little harder to find a spiritual root for my ornament shaped like a baseball or the dried okra snowman, but I believe you can look at a Christmas tree and see it as a visual prayer of thanksgiving—a reminder of the things that make our lives interesting and rich, a way of showing gratitude for the life God gave us.

As you go through this week, it might help you to recall the happiest Christmas you remember. What made it such a fine celebration? Consider how the events of that Christmas contributed to your emotions and patterned your hopes for what Christmas can be. What brings joy for you? How can you share it?

fourth sunday of advent

SING FOR JOY

THIS IS THE FOURTH SUNDAY OF ADVENT. CHRISTMAS is just around the corner. Our celebration is about to begin, and a main feature of Christmas celebrations all over the world is music. Singing is a wonderful way to pray with the body. When we sing with emotion and conviction, our whole body responds with chemical and physical reactions. Our brain releases endorphins and our muscles relax. We glow. Some people will object that singing does not release such pleasure in them because they can't sing, don't carry a tune, and so forth. But this is not about performance, it's about prayer. One way the Bible calls for us to worship God is by making a joyful noise.

Pick out two Christmas carols to sing. Choose one set in a minor key, a song of longing for God's redemption to draw near, like "O Come, O Come Emmanuel" or "Let All Mortal Flesh Keep Silence," which is very much about incarnation. Sing this song as an invitation for Christ to be born afresh in your heart, for God to redeem humanity and make all things new. Then, choose a joyful hymn like "Joy to the World" or "The First Noel," and sing it with as much vigor as you can muster. Make it a prayer of adoration, an exultation.

Could you feel your sense of well-being rise with your singing? Do you agree that singing is prayer? Why or why not? What emotions or thoughts do you want to express to God that you cannot say in song? Can you imagine a prayerful mood you express in song that you can't quite put into words? What songs—whether originally written as religious music or secular music—are among your most treasured spiritual experiences? Make a list of your all-time favorites, and sing or listen to one of them today.

11

now and always

READ Psalm 90:1-10

ONE WAY TO CELEBRATE ADVENT IS TO OBSERVE THE passage of time as a spiritual practice. We do this with Advent calendars and Advent wreaths, counting down the days from the first Sunday in Advent to Christmas Eve, lighting candles, opening windows, anchoring ourselves in each day and pointing our awareness toward the special day that is coming. This practice reminds us that we are in time and out of time, that God's presence in the world is right here and now and also eternal, already and not yet.

I heard about a way of marking Advent time from a friend who had a lovely nativity scene, one with lots of animals and a wooden stable with real hay on the floor. She sets up the scene a few figures at a time, first placing the animals in the stable, then Mary and Joseph, then angels, then shepherds, then on December 24, the baby himself. But she still isn't finished, because there are the kings. If you read the biblical accounts of the Nativity carefully, you see that Luke tells the story of Jesus' birth with Mary and Joseph having to go to Bethlehem, there being no room in the inn, and the shepherds being summoned by the angels—the familiar story we retell every year. But the wise men come from Matthew's story of Jesus, and the story really differs. Many of us meld the stories together and put the Magi right there in the stable. Since this is not a history project, I say anything goes. But technically the Magi aren't supposed to show up until January 6, the feast of the Epiphany, which happens twelve days after Christmas.

My friend sets her Magi on the road toward Bethlehem by placing them somewhere in another part of the house, away from the nativity scene. Each day she and her children move them a little closer to the stable, up a bookshelf, across a table, down the hall from one room to another, making a little journey to symbolize the journey the wise men took following that star.

This tradition of creating a journey for the Magi seems to me a charming way to observe the passage of time and the progress of the story, to make it take on some reality in our imagination. Perhaps it appeals to me because it's an exercise in incarnation, a practice of anchoring the story we know so well in physical movements that help us connect the Magi's journey to the journey we must take to the manger to kneel before the Christ child and offer what we have. Our Advent practices also offer a way of incarnating time, of giving a physical, visual dimension to a concept we cannot see or touch.

Where is your sense of holy time in the Advent season? Are you scrambling to catch up with a list of chores? Are you wondering how to find that elusive sense of the Christmas spirit? Finding a few minutes each day to sit in God's presence can help you feel calmer and more festive too. It may be a little late in the season to start an Advent calendar if you haven't already but consider how you might work with the passage of time over this next week. You might try moving the Magi around the house if you have a nativity. You might burn a candle during an evening time of prayer, preferably a slender candle where a half hour's burning will make a noticeable change in its size after each period of use. Note what associations or memories this candle burning evokes for you. Experience time as a gift, moving us deeper and deeper into the heart of incarnation.

~ Ask ~

Do you remember the days before Christmas moving with incredible slowness when you were a child? Is your current sense of time marked by how much you have to do in the coming days or by what you look forward to enjoying in the future?

~ Pray ~

God of the eternal now, help us to see time as another of your gifts to us, which we can experience as a form of grace and a window into your eternal nature.

iii

pray with your senses

READ Isaiah 35:1-10

To truly celebrate the Feast of the Incarnation, we have to put our incarnation into the feast. That means allowing your body to be an avenue of prayer, the location of the work of spiritual formation. One way to do this comes in praying with your senses, using the five physical senses to heighten your awareness of God's presence in your world.

Consider for a moment all the sensory information that will likely pass through you as you celebrate Christmas: the sight of your Christmas tree, decked with lights and symbols that have meaning to you and your family; the smell of evergreen or candle wax or cookies baking; the taste of that cookie or an orange or peppermint; the sound of carols sung in small groups or accompanied by an organ filling a church; the brush of a loved one's hand as the flame passes from one candle to another at a Christmas Eve service.

We undergo a complex process when we consider one bit of sensory data and translate that into symbol, metaphor, prayer. We behold the object, and our sight identifies it—a candle, for example. Our brain does some quick work that tells us if the candle is a one-dimensional picture of a candle or a real object; our sense of smell and touch tell us if the flame is real fire or electric. Our knowledge of the context fills in the details: this burning candle in church on a Sunday in Advent does more than give light; it reminds us that Christ is the Light of the world. Our mind takes us on a tour of the ways light has meaning, from the first day of Creation to the star shining in the east. When have we felt enlightened? When have we groped painfully in the dark?

The power of metaphor lies in the way it fuses experience and language, the particular and the universal. Our senses are the way this process begins, the first link in the chain of taking in the clues to the presence of the holy in the ordinary.

My mother felt that a bayberry candle was the absolute essence of Christmas. I still remember her delight at getting out that fragrant green candle as part of our decorating ritual and the heady scent that would fill the house when the flame took hold. This year I set out to buy a bayberry candle of my own, but I could not find one. At the stores I visited, I found scented candles of overblown pine-nutmeg-wassail combinations, but the pure scent of something as simple as bayberry seemed out of the question. When I find that candle, I know its smell will instantly transport me to past Christmases that live inside me, their stories intact—the year of the big snow, the year of the pink knee-socks, the tropical Christmas when we went to the beach.

For the next few days the Christmas essence will bombard your senses. You may have become slightly immune to it. Today seek to engage one of your senses as an act of prayer. Drink in the memories that might flood back to you. Focus on the spiritual connection the physical sense can offer. Give thanks for your body, which brings you the good news of God's presence in every moment. Let each of your senses in turn give you its unique version of the good news so that together the Feast of the Incarnation lives in you in all its richness and splendor.

~ Ask ~

What does Christmas smell like? taste like? Which of the senses is the easiest to understand as a form of prayer? the hardest? What can you do today to engage each of your senses in a form of prayer?

~ Pray ~

God, we praise you for each of the gifts you have given us in our senses. Let them be our deep, powerful, continual source of awareness of your presence.

shepherds and angels

READ Luke 2:8-20

AT THE NATIVITY OF JESUS, THE WITNESSES WERE angels and shepherds, the cast of so many church Christmas pageants, saying their lines about the wondrous sights they beheld that night in Bethlehem. These two groups represent the highest and the lowest order of creation, the spirit and the flesh.

Popular culture sometimes depicts angels as departed humans who have risen up through the ranks in heaven. I am not sure the Bible supports that idea. Angels in the Bible seem to be divine beings. Since they appear in recognizable forms to humans, we might even see them as a bridge between humanity and divinity, a half step toward incarnation.

Angels seem to serve as God's messengers, bringing tidings of joy, warning, comfort, and challenge. An angel brought the news of Mary's pregnancy to her and foretold the gift this child would be. Angels appear at Jesus' birth again and reveal to the shepherds what has occurred.

Angels will minister to Jesus after his long forty days in the desert that began his ministry, and they stand at the tomb when the first witnesses arrive. The angels are a part of things humans can't see and don't know, the spiritual realms we can't attain, the mysteries of God's miracles and interventions, the wisdom of eternity.

Shepherds represent one of the bottom rungs of biblical society. They are among the poorest and least powerful. They lived with their flocks in rough conditions for long stretches of time. Their work kept them outside and away from the Temple, kept them from the regular services and rituals. They probably saw a great deal from their perches on the hillsides overlooking the towns of Judea. They surely were well acquainted with the night sky. Their wisdom was practical, built on experience and patience. They signify what is mortal, fleshly, a little dirty and weary, but also connected to life at its core, to birth and death and the turning of the seasons, the wisdom of time.

We inhabit lives that are part angel, part shepherd. We have the life of the field and flock, our work to do, our charges to keep. We know the physical life of fatigue and grime and managing the relationships with our coworkers and our families. We have wisdom gathered from experiences and seasons and lots of trial and error. But we also carry with us a little of the angels. Maybe in our dreams we receive glimpses of things we half understand, images and whispers and coincidences, things we know from some mysterious source that we don't even know how to speak about and might try to deny. We possess a sense of God that must have been given to us by God, because it seems hardwired, innate, a gift.

Those shepherds must have had a lot of time to think about such matters. Some of them maybe said it had all been a dream, but the ones who had been there—they knew. They had seen the child, just like the angels had said. They had heard the singing, and they hoped they might hear it again someday. The angels had told them not to be afraid and somehow, now, they were not.

Our celebration of Christmas needs a little angel and a little shepherd in it. We need to sing the *gloria in excelsis Deo*—the music of the stars—and be lifted up into the transcendent moment. And then we need to go back to our fields, to be like shepherds, to ponder what we have seen and how it will change us.

~ Ask ~

When have you felt you were in the presence of the holy? What set that time apart from everyday life—was it a sound, an inner knowing, or something suddenly clear in a book or a song? How is this wisdom the same and not the same as the wisdom of daily life?

~ Pray ~

Let us be aware of your approach, God of angels and shepherds. Let us attend to your revelation through mystery and matter.

ooooo

lasting lessons

READ 2 Kings 22:8-20

ONE THEME OF THIS BOOK IS TO URGE YOU TO SEE
yourself as an incarnation. While it may be true we are
not incarnations in the full sense that Jesus was, it is
nevertheless true that the Bible depicts humans as being
made in the image of God and carrying the divine spark.
Your incarnation is unique, unrepeatable, irreplaceable,
somehow necessary to the kingdom. That means that your
story with all its bumps and bruises, your disappointments
and failures as well as your shining essence of gifts and
graces, is hallowed by God's investment in incarnation. We
carry our story into our Christmas celebration, into the
traditions we keep and the ones we reinterpret or transform
or allow ourselves to end.

When my widowed father remarried, a whole new set
of siblings entered my life. In their previous life as a family
they had a whole different way of "doing Christmas," so
our first few Christmases together were a little rocky.

Painful reminders about the losses we had experienced went into this blended family. But we made some new traditions together beginning with the request my sister Beth made one Christmas morning for cheeseburgers for breakfast. Because Beth had been sick for weeks and had missed most of the Christmas goodie consumption, my stepmother granted Beth's unorthodox request. We kept that menu as Christmas brunch fare for many years.

Do you know where your traditions came from? How does your family's ethnic heritage play a part? How does the history of migration alter and extend the traditions? We take some small things for granted about how Christmas is done—the sorts of ornaments we put on our trees, or what we do on Christmas Eve and what we save for Christmas Day. These traditions might reflect where our ancestors came from and the challenges they faced as they chose how much to assimilate and how much to remain connected to the traditions they brought with them.

These stories from our past are not unbroken lines that arrive neatly wrapped. There are breaks, lost stories, tragedies. We are shaped by legacies of war, slavery, family conflict, and the necessities of survival. In the story from today's suggested scripture reading found in Second Kings, Josiah has ordered a repair of the Temple. The high priest Hilkiah finds a scroll that describes the covenant God made with Israel, a covenant the people have forgotten, betrayed, broken. Josiah's first response to the discovery is grief. He realizes the loss of having been chosen by God for relationship and then allowing that relationship to fall away like an old friend we have lost touch with. King Josiah sends priests to the prophetess Huldah, and she serves him words of warning and of comfort about what is still to come. Despite the sad truth of Huldah's prophecy,

Josiah does not waver in faith. He organizes a ceremony for the people to renew the covenant and reconcile the relationship.

Our celebrations of Christmas are part of an ongoing pattern that recognizes our relationship with God. Even some of the small things we can do with our eyes closed—singing carols or lighting a candle—contribute to maintaining the relationship, upholding the covenant. As you perform rituals this season, give thanks for your ancestors who played their part in the story that brought you here and nourished you. And give thanks for our ancestors like Josiah and Huldah who had the gifts of discernment and courage to reveal the hidden workings of God's kingdom and call us to repentance and change.

~ Ask ~

How faithfully do you duplicate family traditions and how freely do you update them? What one aspect of your Christmas celebration feels the most important?

~ Pray ~

For all that has been, we give you thanks, Rock of Ages. And for all that will be, we pledge to play our part with gratitude and courage and hope.

ᶦ ᶦ ᶦ ᶦ ᶦ ᶦ

mystery and meaning

READ Philippians 2:6-11

INCARNATION IS ABOUT PARADOX—THE HOLDING together of two ideas that on the surface seem to be mutually exclusive. The idea of Jesus as fully human and fully divine requires us to hold together two ideas that seem incompatible. In the spiritual realm, we call this *mystery*—a lovely word that has an unfortunate connection to whodunits and detectives and forensic evidence. But mystery, in its spiritual sense, is not about a puzzle to be solved but about meaning that continually unfolds. Mystery is the well of God's revelation to us and for us, a well that is bottomless, ageless, limitless. We always have more to discover. We can try to resolve our spiritual paradoxes intellectually. We can pray for the grace to believe them spiritually. In the end, however, the paradox will remain—two magnetic field poles full of energy and light in a perpetual dance.

Our bodies themselves are a mystery. Science still doesn't know how the brain works or how the animating force makes our hearts beat. Our bodies are incredibly strong and yet curiously vulnerable. We can recover from having our hearts opened up and stitched back together and then be felled by a tiny microbe we can't see. Our inner dimensions follow a similar pattern. Humans have the capacity to invent and build amazing things, yet we can be tripped up by our own hubris and greed.

I see evidence of a curious paradox in the way many of us employ technology, especially our mobile devices. These cell phones and tablet computers allow us to contact people on the other side of the world, to be in touch with the history unfolding around us in ways that are faster, more precise, and more intimate than has ever been possible. And yet, as I watch people in restaurants and stores, all absorbed in their own devices, it seems that the way most of us use this technology cuts us off from one form of communication even as it enables another.

How did Jesus understand the paradox of incarnation? The writer of Philippians includes an ancient bit of poetry, maybe a scrap of a hymn that honors Christ as both having equality with God and embracing the role of servant, of accepting the human death he suffered and becoming eternally exalted. We celebrate this paradox at Christmas; we celebrate a helpless baby as a king and proclaim a poor child in a backwater town as Light of the world.

Our Christmas celebrations hint at this paradox, suggesting a deeper reason behind the urge to drag a green plant inside our house in the middle of winter. Look around your home at the symbols of Christmas you see. Which represent the powerful, strong side of the Christian paradox, the kingly realm? Which represent Jesus in his poverty and vulnerability? Find or, if necessary, make two such symbols: one about your vulnerability, your dependence on God, your weakness, your poverty, or your brokenness and the other about your power, strength, spiritual gift, blessedness. Hang them on your tree, put them in your Bible, or paste them on your fridge where you will see them and be reminded of this mystery we celebrate and carry within us. As you embrace the paradox of incarnation, let your prayer be that it will unfold and deepen as you continue to live out the union of body and spirit and walk the way of Christ.

~ ASK ~

Make a quick inventory of what you carry in your pockets, purse, or bag. How do these items represent both your power and your vulnerability? Which item would be the hardest to let go of? Why?

~ PRAY ~

As we bend our knees to honor you, Lord Christ, as our tongues confess your glory, give us a glimpse of your humility that we may see our own path of self-giving.

emmanuel, god with us

READ John 1:1-14

MERRY CHRISTMAS! WE HAVE ARRIVED AT THE DAY our Advent preparations were leading us toward, the Feast of the Incarnation, the joyful proclamation that God has chosen not merely to observe or direct human affairs but to participate in them, to invest in our future in the most intimate terms.

After these weeks of considering what the Incarnation teaches us about God and what it teaches us about human life, after considering how Jesus lived his incarnation as an example for ours, we are now ready to bring it all together in a celebration of joy: a day to worship, to honor the body, to practice hospitality, and to tell the old story once again. Celebrating the Incarnation, holding up its gifts and lessons, will allow us to enter into the spirit of Christmas, observing our traditions of meals and gift-giving and small family rituals.

Yes, at times commercialism and greed outrageously compromise Christmas. Many of us carry impossible expectations for family harmony and togetherness that will be disappointed. And tomorrow we may have to return to work or out to shovel snow or to sort out bills with the deflated sense that all our special effort was barely noticed. But at its core, Christmas encompasses far more than our efforts to achieve an ideal. It is about boundless love and redemptive grace. It exists to express joy, the joy that floods us when we know that God is close by and always will be.

Now Advent gives way to the Christmas season and then shortly on to Epiphany. The season of Epiphany relates to the insight, the realization of the Magi when they beheld Jesus and understood who he was and why they had made the long journey to find him. During Epiphany we also celebrate the Baptism of the Lord, another moment when Jesus' identity was revealed in a powerful way through a voice coming down from heaven.

The days between today and Epiphany, January 6, represent the fabled twelve days of Christmas. The celebration of Christmas continues during these twelve days. The Christmas tree stays up; the carols are still sung; the colors of the church paraments don't change. While some of us are no doubt chomping at the bit to take down the tree and get the house back to normal, there may be value in extending our observance long enough to let the message of the Incarnation soak into our daily lives, into our understandings of our nature, until some epiphanies appear.

We might ask ourselves what insights have emerged over these last weeks, ponder how we have grown spiritually, and wonder if that growth is calling us to make changes or try anything new in the weeks and months to come. What new spiritual disciplines do we want to explore? What relationships need tending? What do we want to pray for and about? Have we gained a fresh understanding of our particular story, the twists and turns along the way, the losses and gains, the small moments of intense connection that have brought us here? We can hold these close and celebrate them as a fitting blessing and benediction on this day.

~ Ask ~

What insights from this Advent exploration do you want to carry into the coming seasons? What one prayer or action can remind you of its significance?

~ Pray ~

For the gifts you have given us, we are grateful, O God. For the gifts we can give to others, we give you thanks. For the love that binds it all, we lift our hearts. Amen.

study guide

THIS GUIDE WILL IS SERVE AS A RESOURCE FOR SMALL groups who want to explore the ideas in *Embodied Light* as a form of corporate spiritual formation. The guide's structure has six sessions: an introductory meeting for organizing the group and getting to know one another, four meetings to coincide with the four Sundays in Advent and the four sections of this book, and a final session for summing up the process and reviewing the group's experience. Each session will take about an hour. Your group members should covenant together about the time you will spend and try to honor that commitment. If your group chooses, you might schedule a meal together before or after each session or after the final session to complete the group's time together. Each session needs a leader to facilitate the process of the discussion. Your group might choose to rotate this responsibility among its members. Each group leader should consider the preparation needed to lead the group, both outwardly, considering the need to prepare the meeting space, including any supplies noted in the meeting outline as well as inward preparation, praying for each member of the group that this meeting time will be an experience of grace. If the group size is larger than ten, it might be advisable during the discussion of each session's activity to form groups of three or four for sharing responses.

SESSION ONE

Gathering (about 20 minutes)

Spend this time getting to know one another a little better. Share your names and one thing Advent means to you or one thing you look forward to doing during Advent.

Discussing (30 minutes)

Have a group member read the poem by Mary Oliver that serves as the prologue to the book. Sit for a few minutes in silence and then read the poem again.

Use the following questions to guide a discussion of this poem:

- What does the poet mean when she writes that the spirit longs "to be more than pure light that burns where no one is"?
- Why does the spirit need "the metaphor of the body"?
- What does the word *metaphor* mean to you in this context?
- How do you feel when you read of the "dark hug of time"? How is this a positive image? How is it negative?
- What sorts of things do you experience as "brute comfort"?

After this discussion, read the poem again and then sit for a few moments in silence.

Now ask this question: Why do you think this book might be titled *Embodied Light*? In what way do you feel that each of us human beings is embodied light?

Planning (10 minutes)

Before ending the time together, take a few minutes to organize the sessions for the coming weeks. If you decide to share the leadership roles, ask who will serve for the next week. Make sure everyone has a copy of the book or knows how to get one before next week. Agree that for the next session members will read the meditation for each day and come prepared to share which meditations in that week's readings were particularly meaningful or less helpful. Ask members to bring personal journals or writing paper and writing utensils. Mention that the Sunday meditations for each week include a body prayer experience, a form of prayer that recognizes the human body as a place where the Spirit dwells. Encourage members to engage these Sundays prayerfully as part of their preparation.

Close the session with prayer.

Session Two

Gathering (20 minutes)

Greet one another and take a few minutes to reflect on the readings for the First Week of Advent. Which meditation had the most meaning for you? Which one raised questions? How did you process those questions during the week?

Discussing (30 minutes)

The introduction to this week suggests that the readings will consider what the Incarnation tells us about God. Use the following questions to guide reflection:

- How did you first learn about God? How has your mind changed as you have grown and learned? What ideas about what God is like have remained the most constant?
- Do you think of God as an old white man with a long gray beard? Why or why not?
- How do you imagine God when you pray?
- What words would you use to describe God?

Have each member take a piece of paper and write on the top:

"What I know about God." Then add these columns:

From Nature   **From Scripture**   **From My Experience**

Spend about five minutes writing down what comes to mind for each of these sections.

Then share in the group any of these ideas, as members feel comfortable.

Closing (10 minutes)

To close this meeting, practice the gesture prayer (page 16) explained in the meditation for the first Sunday of Advent. Do it several times until it becomes a smoothly flowing gesture.

SESSION THREE

Gathering (20 minutes)

Greet one another and take a few minutes to reflect on the readings for the Second Week of Advent. Which meditation had the most meaning for you? Which one raised questions? How did you process those questions during the week?

Discussing (30 minutes)

The introduction to this week suggests that we consider what the Incarnation teaches us about being human. Use these questions to guide the discussion:

- What makes humans different from other animals?
- How does sin alienate us from God? What can reconcile us? Is sin a curse or an unavoidable result of freedom? Do you understand it through the model of sickness and health or legal rights and consequences? Why or why not?
- Can you think of Jesus as both human and divine? What is the harder part of that equation for you?
- Can you see yourself as an incarnation? How?
- How comfortable are you with the idea of celebrating your incarnation?
- What might make you more comfortable with this idea?

Have a member of the group read Genesis 1:1-3. How do these verses suggest the idea that God spoke the world into existence? Now read John 1:1-4 and verse 14. How is this passage similar to Genesis 1? How is it different? In one of this week's meditations, the writer Robert Mulholland is quoted as saying that each of us is a word spoken forth into being for the sake of the world. Take one or two minutes to sit quietly with the question: What word was I spoken forth to become for the sake of the world? Share your answers with the group as you are comfortable. If a group member has trouble claiming herself or himself as a word spoken forth by God for the sake of the world, other group members could share a spiritual gift they see in that member that might inspire a possible answer.

Closing (10 minutes)

Use the gesture prayer (page 16) as the closing prayer for this session. Ask group members if there are particular prayer concerns they would like to lift up in the final prayer. Remind the group that the movements of their hands and arms are movements of the prayer, lifting up our needs before God and opening us to the movement of the Spirit. Repeat the gesture prayer several times.

SESSION FOUR

Gathering (20 minutes)

Greet one another and take a few minutes to reflect on the readings for the Third Week of Advent. Which meditation had the most meaning for you? Which one raised questions? How did you process those questions during the week?

Discussing (30 minutes)

This week's meditations focused on Jesus and how his life shows us how to love God and neighbor. The meditations for each day were headed by the following brief imperative phrases. Have someone write them on a whiteboard or newsprint pad:

Go Deep

Face Temptation

Practice Hospitality

Befriend God

Be Poor

Forgive and Be Forgiven

Use these questions to guide a discussion:

These phrases are offered as a set of answers to the question: How do I love God and neighbor? What would you add to this list? What would you change or improve? What would you omit?

Consider the idea that these phrases could be used as a prayer.

Go through the Lord's Prayer line by line and match up phrases from the list the group has just edited. Which phrases on your list echo an idea from the Lord's Prayer? Do any seem disconnected or in contradiction? Why or why not? Create a prayer that includes phrases from the list of meditation themes and phrases from the Lord's Prayer.

Closing (10 minutes)

Pray your completed prayer together as a closing.

Note: before leaving this session, announce that the next session requires a bit of preparation. Ask members of the group to divide up the following list so that each person brings one item that completes one of these statements:

Christmas smells like _____

Christmas tastes like _____

Christmas sounds like _____

Christmas feels like _____

Christmas looks like _____

(If you have fewer than five members of the group, ask one or more members to bring two items).

SESSION FIVE

Gathering (20 minutes)

Greet one another and take a few minutes to reflect on the readings for the Fourth Week of Advent. Which meditation had the most meaning for you? Which one raised questions? How did you process those questions during the week?

Discussing (35 minutes)

This week's meditations focused on celebrating Christmas as the Feast of the Incarnation. This session will use our physical senses to consider how we can bring our incarnational powers to the celebration. Ask each member to show the item he or she brought in and explain how that item completes the phrases:

Christmas smells like _____
Christmas tastes like _____
Christmas sounds like _____
Christmas feels like _____
Christmas looks like _____

Spend about five minutes with each item, savoring the smells, sounds, etc. Briefly offer stories or memories that connect to that sense. How is your sense of Christmas the same or different from the other group members? How many of these connections were forged in your childhood? Later? How are your physical senses connected to a spiritual wisdom?

Closing (5 minutes)

End the session by singing a Christmas carol together.

SESSION SIX

Gathering (20 minutes)

Greet one another and take a few minutes to reflect on what this Advent experience has meant to you. How did the daily reading of the meditations change your experience of Advent? of Christmas? What one meditation stuck out among all the rest? Why did that particular meditation speak to you? Were there any scripture passages you will now understand in a new light?

Discussing (30 minutes)

Have a member of the group read the Mary Oliver poem with which we began this study.

How has your understanding of this poem changed over the last six weeks?

How have your ideas about the Incarnation changed?

What most challenged you?

What most comforted you?

What do you want to take with you as part of the next season of your spiritual life?

Closing (20 minutes)

End this session by blessing one another. Stand in a circle and ask each member as she or he feels led to step into the center of the circle. While there, members of the group will participate in the laying on of hands, an old Christian practice of blessing. Members of the group will together place a hand on the shoulder, arm or head of the person in the center. Offer brief prayers of thanksgiving for that person, for the word they were spoken forth to be, for the way they are an incarnation. Allow room for silence and for all members who wish to pray to do so. Continue until each person has had a chance to step inside the circle and be blessed.

Notes

Frontispiece
Mary Oliver, "Poem," *Dream Work* (New York: Atlantic Monthly Press, 1986), 52.

Introduction
1. Rubem Alves, *I Believe in the Resurrection of the Body*, trans. L. M. McCoy, 2nd ed. (Minneapolis, MN: Fortress Press, 1986), 7–8.

Week One
1. Langston Hughes, "Dream Dust," *Selected Poems of Langston Hughes* (New York: Vintage, 1990), 75.
2. M. Robert Mulholland, *Shaped by the Word* (Nashville, TN: Upper Room Books, 1985), 34–38.
3. www.guardian.co.uk/science/2010/sep/19/scientists-prune-world-plant-list
4. Gerard Manley Hopkins, "As Kingfishers Catch Fire," *God's Grandeur and Other Poems* (Mineola, NY: Dover Publications, 1995), 37.

Week Two
1. www.answers.com/topic/anatomy
2. Irenaeus of Lyons, *Against Heresies, Ante-Nicene Fathers*, vol. I, Alexander Roberts and James Donaldson (eds.) (Peabody, MA: Hendrickson Publishers, 1994), 490.
3. Tertullian, *Against Marcion, Ante-Nicene Fathers*, vol. III, Alexander Roberts and James Donaldson (eds.) (Peabody, MA: Hendrickson Publishers, 1994), 329.

Week Three
1. Terence, *The Self-Tormentor, The Complete Comedies of Terence* (Rutgers, NJ: Rutgers University Press, 1974), 84, line 74.
2. C. S. Lewis, *The Last Battle* (New York: The Macmillan Company, 1966), 163.